YOUR COMPLETE CAPRICORN 2025 PERSONAL HOROSCOPE

Monthly Astrological Prediction Forecast Readings of Every Zodiac Astrology Sun Star Signs- Love, Romance, Money, Finances, Career, Health, Travel Spirituality.

Iris Quinn

Alpha Zuriel Publishing

Your Complete Capricorn 2025 Personal Horoscope/ Iris Quinn. -- 1st ed.

"Astrology is a language. If you understand this language, the sky speaks to you."

— IRIS QUINN

CONTENTS

C H A P T E R O N E

CAPRICORN PROFILE

General Characteristics

- **Element:** Earth
- **Quality:** Cardinal
- **Ruler:** Saturn
- **Symbol:** The Goat
- **Dates:** December 22 - January 19

Personality Traits

- **Disciplined:** Known for their strong sense of duty and responsibility.
- **Ambitious:** Highly driven to achieve their goals.
- **Practical:** Focused on realistic and tangible outcomes.
- **Patient:** Willing to work hard over the long term to achieve success.
- **Reserved:** Often appear serious and composed.
- **Determined:** Unwavering in their pursuit of their objectives.

- **Cautious:** Carefully considers all options before making decisions.
- **Loyal:** Deeply committed to their loved ones and responsibilities.
- **Organized:** Excel at planning and managing resources effectively.
- **Resourceful:** Capable of making the most of any situation.

Strengths

- **Persistence:** Willing to put in the necessary work to achieve long-term goals.
- **Reliability:** Dependable and trustworthy in fulfilling commitments.
- **Practicality:** Focused on achieving realistic and meaningful results.
- **Discipline:** Maintains a strong sense of self-control and responsibility.
- **Leadership:** Natural ability to guide and manage others effectively.
- **Wisdom:** Makes decisions based on careful thought and experience.

Weaknesses

- **Pessimism:** Can sometimes focus too much on potential difficulties.
- **Stubbornness:** May be unwilling to change or adapt.
- **Reserved Nature:** Can appear distant or unapproachable.
- **Overworking:** Tendency to prioritize work over personal life.

- **Rigidity:** May struggle with flexibility and spontaneity.
- **Self-criticism:** Can be overly hard on themselves.

Planets and Their Influences

- **Career Planet:** Saturn – Emphasizes discipline, structure, and long-term goals.
- **Love Planet:** Venus – Governs affection, beauty, and relationships.
- **Money Planet:** Saturn – Focuses on financial responsibility and long-term planning.
- **Planet of Fun, Entertainment, Creativity, and Speculations:** Jupiter – Encourages optimism and joy.
- **Planet of Health and Work:** Mercury – Influences communication and routine.
- **Planet of Home and Family Life:** Moon – Governs emotions and domestic affairs.
- **Planet of Spirituality:** Neptune – Represents dreams and intuition.
- **Planet of Travel, Education, Religion, and Philosophy:** Jupiter – Governs expansion and learning.

Compatibility

- **Signs of Greatest Overall Compatibility:** Taurus, Virgo
- **Signs of Greatest Overall Incompatibility:** Aries, Libra
- **Sign Most Supportive for Career Advancement:** Scorpio

- **Sign Most Supportive for Emotional Well-being:** Pisces
- **Sign Most Supportive Financially:** Cancer
- **Sign Best for Marriage and/or Partnerships:** Taurus
- **Sign Most Supportive for Creative Projects:** Virgo
- **Best Sign to Have Fun With:** Gemini
- **Signs Most Supportive in Spiritual Matters:** Pisces
- **Best Day of the Week:** Saturday

Additional Details

- **Colors:** Black, Dark Brown
- **Gem:** Garnet
- **Scent:** Pine, Cypress
- **Birthstone:** Garnet
- **Quality:** Cardinal (initiates and leads)

PERSONALITY OF CAPRICORN

Capricorn, ruled by Saturn and symbolized by the Goat, is known for its grounded, pragmatic approach to life. Born between December 22 and January 19, Capricorns are deeply rooted in the earth element, which imparts a sense of realism, determination, and a strong connection to the material world. They are often seen as the most serious and disciplined of the zodiac signs, with an inherent drive to achieve their goals and climb the metaphorical mountains of success and recognition.

A defining trait of Capricorn is their ambition. From a young age, Capricorns are driven by a desire to succeed and are often focused on long-term goals. This ambition is not merely about personal gain; it is deeply intertwined with their sense of responsibility and duty. Capricorns feel a strong obligation to provide for themselves and their loved ones, and this often manifests in their careers, where they strive for excellence and leadership positions. They are willing to put in the hard work and dedication required to achieve their objectives, often displaying an impressive level of persistence and resilience.

Capricorns are known for their practicality and realistic outlook on life. They have a keen ability to assess situations and make decisions based on logic and practicality rather than emotion. This pragmatic approach allows them to navigate challenges effectively and find solutions that are both feasible and beneficial in the long run. Capricorns are excellent planners, always thinking ahead and preparing for potential obstacles. This foresight and careful planning often lead to their success, as they are rarely caught off guard by unexpected events.

Despite their outwardly serious demeanor, Capricorns possess a deep and often understated sense of humor. Their wit is typically dry and subtle, and they enjoy clever wordplay and irony. This sense of humor is a hidden gem, revealing itself to those who take the time to get to know them beyond their initial reserve. Capricorns are often more relaxed and playful in private, showing a side of themselves that is warm, affectionate, and deeply loyal to those they care about.

In relationships, Capricorns are devoted and reliable partners. They take their commitments seriously and are known for their loyalty and steadfastness. While they may not be the most overtly romantic sign, they express their love through actions rather than words. A Capricorn will show their affection by being there when needed, providing support, and ensuring their partner feels secure and cared for. They value stability and consistency in their relationships and seek partners who share these values.

One of the challenges Capricorns face is their tendency towards pessimism and self-criticism. Their high standards and drive for perfection can lead them to be overly hard on themselves, often feeling like they are not doing enough or falling short of their goals. This can sometimes manifest as a reluctance to take risks or step out of their comfort zones. Capricorns benefit from learning to balance their practical nature with a bit of spontaneity and self-compassion, allowing themselves to enjoy the journey rather than focusing solely on the destination.

Capricorns also have a strong sense of duty and responsibility, which can sometimes make them appear reserved or distant. They prioritize their obligations and may struggle to relax and let go of their worries. However, once they feel secure and confident in their achievements, they can become more open and willing to share their inner world with others.

In essence, the personality of Capricorn is a blend of ambition, practicality, and loyalty. They are driven by a desire to achieve and provide, using their realistic and grounded approach to navigate life's challenges. While they may appear serious and reserved, they possess a hidden depth of humor and warmth that is revealed to those who earn their trust. Balancing their ambitious nature with a sense of enjoyment and self-compassion can help Capricorns lead fulfilling and well-rounded lives, both personally and professionally.

WEAKNESSES OF CAPRICORN

As an astrologer, delving into the weaknesses of Capricorn reveals a complex interplay of traits that, while contributing to their strengths, can also pose significant challenges. Capricorns, ruled by Saturn, are known for their ambition, discipline, and pragmatic approach to life. However, these very qualities can sometimes manifest in ways that hinder their personal growth and relationships.

One of the most prominent weaknesses of Capricorn is their tendency towards pessimism. Capricorns are often realistic to a fault, focusing on potential problems and obstacles rather than the possibilities and opportunities. This inclination to anticipate difficulties can lead them to a state of constant worry and anxiety, making it hard for them to enjoy the present moment. Their cautious nature, while useful in planning and avoiding pitfalls, can sometimes prevent them from taking risks and embracing new experiences. They might miss out on opportunities for growth and joy because they are too focused on what could go wrong.

Capricorns are also prone to being overly critical, both of themselves and others. Their high standards and drive for perfection can make them harsh judges, leading to self-criticism that undermines their confidence and self-esteem. They often set unrealistically high expectations for themselves, and when they fall short, they can be exceptionally hard on themselves. This self-critical nature can spill over into their relationships, where they may hold others to the same high standards and become disappointed or frustrated when those expectations are not met. This can create tension and conflict, as those around them may feel they are never quite good enough in the eyes of a Capricorn.

Another challenge for Capricorns is their propensity for workaholism. Their strong sense of duty and responsibility drives them to work tirelessly towards their goals, often at the expense of their personal lives and well-being. They can become so focused on their careers and ambitions that they neglect their need for relaxation, recreation, and connection with loved ones. This relentless pursuit of success can lead to burnout and a sense of isolation, as they sacrifice their personal happiness for professional achievements. Capricorns need to learn to balance their work with leisure and to recognize the importance of taking time for themselves and their relationships.

Capricorns' reserved nature can also be a double-edged sword. While their composure and self-control are admirable, it can sometimes come across as aloofness or emotional distance. They may find it difficult to open up and express their feelings, leading others to perceive them as cold or unapproachable. This can make it challenging for Capricorns to form deep, intimate connections with others. Their fear of vulnerability and rejection can keep them from fully engaging in relationships, both romantic and platonic. Capricorns benefit from learning to trust and to let their guard down, allowing others to see their more sensitive and affectionate side.

Stubbornness is another trait that can work against Capricorns. Once they have made up their mind, they can be inflexible and resistant to change. Their determination to stick to their plans and routines can make it hard for them to adapt to new circumstances or to see different perspectives. This rigidity can limit their ability to grow and evolve, as they may miss out on valuable opportunities for learning and development. Capricorns need to cultivate an openness to change and a willingness to consider alternative viewpoints, which can enhance their personal and professional lives.

Lastly, Capricorns can sometimes be overly materialistic, placing too much importance on financial success and external achievements. Their desire for security and status can lead them to prioritize wealth and career advancement over more meaningful aspects of life, such as personal fulfillment and relationships. This focus on material success can sometimes make them appear superficial or overly concerned with appearances. Capricorns benefit from reminding themselves of the value of intangible rewards, such as love, happiness, and personal growth, and striving for a more balanced and holistic approach to life.

In essence, while Capricorns possess many admirable qualities, their weaknesses often stem from the very traits that make them strong. Their realism can turn into pessimism, their discipline into workaholism, and their high standards into harsh criticism. By recognizing these tendencies and working towards balance and self-compassion, Capricorns can overcome these challenges and lead more fulfilling and harmonious lives.

RELATIONSHIP COMPATIBILITY WITH CAPRICORN

Based only on their Sun signs, this is how Capricorn interacts with others. These are the compatibility interpretations for all 12 potential Capricorn combinations. This is a limited and insufficient method of determining compatibility.

However, Sun-sign compatibility remains the foundation for overall harmony in a relationship.

The general rule is that yin and yang do not get along. Yin complements yin, and yang complements yang. While yin and yang partnerships can be successful, they require more effort. Earth and water zodiac signs are both Yin. Yang is represented by the fire and air zodiac signs.

Capricorn with Yin Signs (Earth and Water)

Capricorn and Taurus (Yin with Yin):

Capricorn and Taurus share a natural compatibility, both being earth signs. Their relationship is grounded in practicality, stability, and mutual respect. Taurus appreciates Capricorn's ambition and work ethic, while Capricorn values Taurus's reliability and loyalty. Both partners are focused on building a secure and comfortable life together, making this a harmonious and enduring match. However, they must guard against becoming too rigid and set in their ways, ensuring they keep the spark alive by trying new things and remaining open to change.

Capricorn and Virgo (Yin with Yin):

The relationship between Capricorn and Virgo is characterized by a strong intellectual and practical connection. Both signs are detail-oriented, disciplined, and value hard work. Virgo's analytical nature complements Capricorn's strategic thinking, making them a powerful team in achieving their goals. They share a deep respect for each other's dedication and reliability, creating a stable and supportive partnership. To maintain harmony, they should make time for relaxation and fun, balancing their work-oriented lives with leisure and enjoyment.

Capricorn and Capricorn (Yin with Yin):

When two Capricorns come together, their relationship is built on mutual understanding and shared values. Both partners are ambitious, disciplined, and focused on long-term success. They support each other in their professional and personal goals, creating a solid foundation for their partnership. However, they must be careful not to let their workaholic tendencies overshadow their relationship. By making an effort to connect emotionally and share quality time, they can build a fulfilling and balanced life together.

Capricorn and Cancer (Yin with Yin):

Capricorn and Cancer have complementary qualities that can create a deeply nurturing and supportive relationship. Capricorn provides the stability and security that Cancer craves, while Cancer offers emotional warmth and care that Capricorn appreciates. Their differences can be a source of strength, as they balance each other's weaknesses. Capricorn's practicality helps ground Cancer's emotions, and Cancer's sensitivity can soften Capricorn's stern exterior. For this relationship to thrive, both partners must be willing to understand and respect their differences, fostering open communication and mutual support.

Capricorn and Scorpio (Yin with Yin):

Capricorn and Scorpio share a powerful and intense connection. Both signs are determined, ambitious, and possess a deep understanding of each other's motivations. Scorpio's passion and emotional depth complement Capricorn's practicality and steadfastness. They can achieve great things together, as Scorpio's intuition and Capricorn's strategic thinking make them a formidable team. However, they must be mindful of their tendency towards control and power struggles. By learning to compromise and respect each other's strengths, they can build a deeply fulfilling and enduring relationship.

Capricorn and Pisces (Yin with Yin):

Capricorn and Pisces have contrasting qualities that can create a balanced and enriching relationship. Capricorn's practicality and discipline provide a stable foundation for Pisces's dreamy and compassionate nature. Pisces offers emotional support and creativity that Capricorn values, while Capricorn provides the structure and security that Pisces needs. Their differences can help them grow and learn from each other, as long as they are willing to communicate openly and appreciate their unique qualities. Capricorn must be patient with Pisces's sensitivity, and Pisces should respect Capricorn's need for order and discipline.

Capricorn with Yang Signs (Fire and Air)

Capricorn and Aries (Yin with Yang):

Capricorn and Aries have contrasting energies that can make their relationship both challenging and rewarding. Aries's spontaneity and enthusiasm can inspire Capricorn to take more risks and embrace new experiences, while Capricorn's practicality and discipline can help ground Aries's impulsive nature. They can learn a lot from each other, but they must be willing to compromise and appreciate their differences. Aries should respect Capricorn's need for structure, and Capricorn should be open to Aries's adventurous spirit. Communication and mutual understanding are key to making this relationship work.

Capricorn and Leo (Yin with Yang):

Capricorn and Leo have different approaches to life that can create both friction and excitement in their relationship. Leo's confidence, warmth, and desire for recognition can clash with Capricorn's reserved and practical nature. However, if they can appreciate each other's strengths, they can form a dynamic partnership. Leo can bring joy and creativity to Capricorn's life, while Capricorn can provide the stability and support that Leo needs. To maintain harmony, they should focus on their common goals and find ways to celebrate each other's successes.

Capricorn and Sagittarius (Yin with Yang):

Capricorn and Sagittarius have contrasting perspectives that can make their relationship a blend of challenges and growth opportunities. Sagittarius's optimism, love for adventure, and desire for freedom can seem at odds with Capricorn's disciplined and structured approach. However, they can complement each other well if they are willing to embrace their differences. Sagittarius can help Capricorn see the bigger picture and enjoy life more, while Capricorn can provide the grounding and focus that Sagittarius needs.

Open communication and a willingness to adapt are essential for making this relationship work.

Capricorn and Gemini (Yin with Yang):

Capricorn and Gemini have very different natures that can create a stimulating but sometimes challenging relationship. Gemini's curiosity, adaptability, and love for variety can contrast with Capricorn's steady and methodical approach. However, if they can find common ground, they can learn a lot from each other. Gemini can bring spontaneity and new ideas to Capricorn's life, while Capricorn can offer stability and practical wisdom to Gemini. Both partners need to be patient and flexible, allowing each other the freedom to express their unique qualities.

Capricorn and Libra (Yin with Yang):

Capricorn and Libra have contrasting but potentially complementary qualities. Libra's charm, diplomacy, and love for harmony can balance Capricorn's seriousness and determination. Libra can help Capricorn relax and enjoy the finer things in life, while Capricorn can provide the stability and direction that Libra needs. Their differences can be a source of growth if they are willing to appreciate and learn from each other. Capricorn should be open to Libra's social nature, and Libra should respect Capricorn's need for structure and discipline.

Capricorn and Aquarius (Yin with Yang):

Capricorn and Aquarius have different approaches to life that can make their relationship both challenging and enriching. Aquarius's innovative, independent, and unconventional nature can contrast with Capricorn's traditional and practical outlook. However, if they can find common ground, they can create a powerful and dynamic partnership. Aquarius can bring fresh perspectives and creativity to Capricorn's life, while Capricorn can offer the stability and focus that Aquarius needs. Open-mindedness and mutual respect are essential for making this relationship work.

In conclusion, Capricorn's compatibility with other sun signs varies widely based on the yin and yang theory. Earth and water signs generally complement Capricorn's practical and disciplined nature, leading to stable and supportive relationships. Fire and air signs, while presenting more challenges, can provide excitement and new perspectives, requiring more effort to navigate their differences. With mutual respect, understanding, and a willingness to learn from each other, Capricorn can form successful and fulfilling partnerships with any sign.

LOVE AND PASSION

Capricorn, an earth sign ruled by Saturn, approaches love and passion with a unique blend of seriousness and depth. Their practical and disciplined nature extends into their romantic lives, where they value stability, commitment, and long-term compatibility. Unlike signs that dive headfirst into the whirlwind of romance, Capricorns take a more measured and thoughtful approach. They believe in building relationships on solid foundations, and this often means taking the time to get to know a partner thoroughly before fully committing.

When a Capricorn falls in love, their dedication is unwavering. They are not the type to be swayed by fleeting emotions or temporary attractions. Instead, they seek partners who can match their level of commitment and who share similar values and life goals. This pragmatic approach to love does not mean that Capricorns lack passion; rather, their passion is expressed in ways that are enduring and profound. They show their love through actions, consistently being there for their partner, and working hard to build a life together that is both secure and fulfilling.

In relationships, Capricorns are known for their loyalty and reliability. They take their promises seriously and will go to great lengths to ensure that they uphold their commitments. This steadfast nature can make their partners feel secure and cherished, knowing that they have someone who will stand by them through thick and thin. Capricorns are not prone to dramatic displays of affection, but their love is demonstrated through their constant presence and the small, thoughtful gestures that show how much they care.

Passion for a Capricorn is often interwoven with their ambition and drive. They are passionate about their goals and aspirations, and they seek partners who can understand and support this aspect of their personality. A Capricorn in love wants to build a future together that is not only emotionally satisfying but also materially secure. They appreciate partners who are equally hardworking and who can contribute to a shared vision of success and stability.

Capricorns also bring a sense of tradition and propriety to their romantic relationships. They value conventional gestures of love and may prefer classic dating rituals over more spontaneous or unconventional displays of affection. This traditional approach can sometimes make them seem reserved or even aloof, but beneath this exterior lies a deep well of emotion and desire. Once a Capricorn feels secure in a relationship, they are capable of great emotional intimacy and warmth.

One of the keys to understanding Capricorn's approach to love is recognizing their need for control and order. They like to plan and organize, ensuring that everything in their lives, including their relationships, runs smoothly. This can sometimes lead to a perception of being overly cautious or even unromantic, but for Capricorns, it is a way of ensuring that their love life is as stable and dependable as the rest of their existence. They believe that a well-ordered relationship is one that can withstand the test of time.

However, Capricorns must be mindful of their tendency to prioritize work and ambition over their personal lives. Their drive for success can sometimes overshadow their need for emotional connection, leading them to neglect their relationships. It is important for Capricorns to strike a balance between their professional and personal lives, making time to nurture their romantic partnerships and show their partners that they are valued and loved.

In terms of passion, Capricorns are often more sensual than they appear. Their reserved exterior hides a deep appreciation for physical intimacy and connection. They are attentive lovers who take the time to understand their partner's needs and desires. For Capricorns, physical closeness is an important expression of love, and they approach it with the same level of dedication and seriousness that they bring to all aspects of their lives.

In conclusion, love and passion for Capricorn are characterized by depth, commitment, and a pragmatic approach. They seek relationships that are built on mutual respect, shared values, and a common vision for the future. While they may not be the most overtly romantic sign, their love is steadfast and enduring, providing a sense of security and stability that is deeply comforting to their partners. By balancing their ambitious nature with a willingness to be emotionally present, Capricorns can create deeply fulfilling and lasting romantic connections.

MARRIAGE

In marriage, Capricorn approaches the union with the same seriousness and dedication they bring to all aspects of their lives. They view marriage as a long-term commitment that requires effort, responsibility, and a shared vision for the future. To keep a Capricorn happy in marriage, it's essential to understand their need for stability, respect, and mutual support.

Capricorns value a strong foundation built on trust and mutual respect. They are not prone to impulsive decisions, and their choice of a life partner reflects careful consideration and a desire for a stable, enduring relationship. They seek partners who are equally committed to the marriage and who share similar goals and values. For Capricorn, marriage is a partnership where both individuals work together towards common objectives, whether those are career achievements, financial security, or raising a family.

Capricorn men in marriage are typically dependable and hardworking. They take their role as a husband seriously, often viewing themselves as the provider and protector of the family. They are ambitious and driven, always striving to improve their circumstances and ensure that their loved ones have everything they need. However, this intense focus on work and achievement can sometimes lead to a tendency to neglect the emotional side of the relationship. Capricorn men need partners who can remind them of the importance of emotional intimacy and who can help them balance their professional aspirations with their personal lives. They appreciate partners who are supportive of their ambitions and who understand the value they place on success and recognition.

Capricorn women in marriage are equally dedicated and industrious. They bring a practical, no-nonsense approach to the union, often taking charge of organizing and managing the household. Capricorn women are known for their resourcefulness and their ability to handle multiple responsibilities with efficiency and grace. They seek partners who can match their level of commitment and who respect their drive and independence. While they may appear reserved, Capricorn women are deeply loyal and nurturing to those they love. They value consistency and reliability in their partners, and they need to feel that their contributions to the marriage are appreciated and reciprocated.

The secret to making a marriage with a Capricorn work lies in understanding and respecting their core values. Capricorns thrive in relationships where there is a clear sense of purpose and direction. They appreciate partners who share their work ethic and who are willing to put in the effort to build a secure and prosperous future together. Open and honest communication is crucial, as Capricorns need to feel that they can discuss their goals, concerns, and expectations without fear of judgment or misunderstanding. They also value a partner who can provide emotional support and who can help them navigate the more challenging aspects of life with patience and understanding.

Capricorns are not naturally inclined towards grand romantic gestures, but they show their love and commitment through their actions. They are dependable and consistent, always willing to go the extra mile to ensure their partner's well-being. To keep a Capricorn happy in marriage, it is important to acknowledge and appreciate these efforts. Small gestures of appreciation and gratitude can go a long way in reinforcing their sense of being valued and loved.

Creating a balance between work and personal life is also essential for maintaining harmony in a marriage with a Capricorn. While they are naturally inclined to focus on their careers and ambitions, Capricorns need to be reminded of the importance of taking time to relax and enjoy life. Encouraging them to take breaks, spend quality time together, and engage in activities that foster emotional connection can help strengthen the bond between partners.

In essence, a successful marriage with a Capricorn is built on mutual respect, shared goals, and a deep commitment to working together through life's challenges. By understanding their need for stability and their drive for success, and by providing the emotional support and appreciation they need, partners can create a fulfilling and enduring relationship with a Capricorn. Their loyalty, dedication, and practical approach to life make them steadfast and reliable partners, capable of building a marriage that stands the test of time.

CHAPTER TWO

CAPRICORN 2025 HOROSCOPE

Overview Capricorn 2025

Capricorn (December 22 - January 19)

Dear Capricorn, 2025 is a year of metamorphosis and renewal for you as the celestial bodies align to support your growth, ambitions, and personal transformation. Prepare to shed old skin and emerge as a more empowered, wise, and authentic version of yourself.

The year begins with a powerful focus on your sign, as the Sun, Mercury, Venus and Pluto are all clustered in Capricorn in January. This stellium amplifies your natural traits of discipline, pragmatism and determination. You'll feel a strong drive to take charge of your life, set ambitious goals, and work diligently towards them. The Capricorn New Moon on January 29 is your cosmic invitation to clarify your intentions and lay the groundwork for the year ahead.

In early February, the conjunction of Saturn and Neptune in Pisces activates your 3rd house of communication, learning and daily environment. This dreamy yet disciplined influence encourages you to infuse more creativity, imagination and compassion into your interactions and thought patterns. It's a favorable time to take up a visionary project, immerse yourself in uplifting studies, or lend a helping hand in your local community.

The pace quickens in March as Mars enters your 6th house of work and wellness, followed by Saturn's ingress into fiery Aries. You'll feel energized to tackle your to-do list, implement healthy routines, and assert yourself in your job. However, Saturn will also square off with Pluto in your sign, demanding that you release any burdens or limits that hold you back from your full potential. It's time to reclaim your power and let your true self shine.

April and May bring opportunities to expand your horizons through travel, higher education, or philosophical pursuits as Jupiter tours your 9th house of wisdom and adventure. This is an auspicious time to broaden your mind, explore new frontiers, and align with your core beliefs. The Lunar Eclipse in Libra on April 12 illuminates your 10th house of career and public image, bringing recognition for your hard work or initiating a shift in your professional path. Trust your instincts and stay true to your values as you navigate any changes.

The middle of the year is marked by a period of introspection and emotional processing as the eclipses activate your 12th house of spirituality and unconscious patterns. The Solar Eclipse in Cancer on June 25 followed by the Lunar Eclipse in Capricorn on July 9 provide a cosmic cleanse, helping you release past traumas, limiting beliefs, and unhealthy attachments. Make space for solitude, self-care, and inner work during this cathartic time. Counseling, journaling, or energy healing can be especially beneficial to integrate any hidden shadows.

As the North Node shifts into Libra and your 10th house in mid-July, your soul's purpose becomes increasingly tied to your calling and contributions in the world. You're primed to step into a leadership role, receive well-deserved accolades, or align your path with humanitarian causes. Let your integrity, wisdom, and dedication to excellence be your guide.

August is a dynamic month as Mars and Venus join forces in your 8th house of intimacy, shared resources, and transformation. You may experience a deepening of a soul connection, explore uncharted depths of your psyche, or undergo a healing crisis that ultimately leads to empowerment. This is an intense time of facing your fears and desires head-on. Honest communication, vulnerability, and emotional alchemization are key.

Come September, the cosmic spotlight returns to your career sector, with a Partial Solar Eclipse in Virgo turbocharging your ambitions and inviting a bold leap towards your dreams. You have the grit, strategic know-how, and unwavering determination to reach new heights. Focus on mastery and respect for your craft. As Mercury stations retrograde in your 10th house, you'll have an opportunity to revise your professional plans and ensure they're built on a solid, intentional foundation.

The last quarter of 2025 emphasizes themes of community, friendship, and collaboration. You may join forces with an exciting new network, deepen your involvement in a humanitarian cause, or receive support from a tribe of kindred spirits. The key is to balance your signature self-reliance with the gifts of interdependence and collective action. Together, you can create remarkable positive change.

As the year comes to a close, Mercury and Venus return to your sign, blessing you with enhanced mental clarity and magnetic charm. You're integrating the immense growth you've undergone and feeling more self-assured than ever. The Capricorn New Moon on December 27 is a beautiful time for reflection and celebration. Take stock of how far you've come and set your sights on even loftier vistas for 2026. You're in the driver's seat of your destiny, Capricorn, and the road ahead is paved with endless possibilities. Trust your resilience, stay anchored in your integrity, and keep climbing towards your highest purpose. The stars are aligned in your favor.

January 2025

Overview Horoscope for the Month:

Happy New Year, Capricorn! January 2025 is set to be a transformative and empowering month for you, as the cosmos align to support your personal growth, ambitions, and new beginnings. With the Sun, Mercury, Venus, and Pluto all converging in your sign at the start of the year, you're feeling a strong sense of purpose, determination, and self-mastery. This is your time to take charge of your life, set clear intentions, and commit to the hard work and discipline required to manifest your goals. The Capricorn New Moon on January 29th serves as a powerful cosmic reset, inviting you to clarify your vision, plant the seeds of your deepest desires, and trust in your ability to create the life you truly want.

Love:

In matters of the heart, January 2025 promises a mix of intensity, passion, and transformation for you, dear Capricorn. The Venus-Pluto conjunction in your sign mid-month brings the potential for profound emotional connections, soulmate encounters, or the deepening of existing bonds. You're craving authentic, meaningful relationships that support your personal growth and empower you to be your best self. This is a time to get radically honest about your desires, needs, and deal-breakers in love. If you're single, you may find yourself magnetically drawn to someone who shares your values, challenges you to grow, and sees the depth of your soul. Trust your instincts and don't settle for anything less than the love you deserve. If you're in a committed partnership, use this potent energy to have vulnerable conversations, deepen your intimacy, and co-create a shared vision for your future together. Remember, true love is not about perfection, but about supporting each other's evolution with compassion, respect, and unwavering commitment.

Career:

Capricorn, your career is set to soar to new heights this month, as the powerful stellium in your sign propels you towards success, recognition, and leadership. You're feeling ambitious, focused, and ready to take on new challenges that showcase your talents and expertise. This is an excellent time to put yourself out there, network with influential people in your field, and make bold moves towards your professional goals. Trust your instincts and don't be afraid to take calculated risks – the universe is conspiring in your favor. Just remember to balance your drive with diplomacy, collaboration, and integrity. Your hard work and dedication will pay off, but make sure your actions align with your values and the greater good. A significant career milestone, promotion, or opportunity could manifest around the New Moon on January 29th. Stay open to the possibilities and know that you have what it takes to succeed.

Finances:

January 2025 is a fantastic month to get your financial house in order, Capricorn. With the Sun, Mercury, Venus, and Pluto all in your sign, you have the focus, discipline, and resourcefulness to create a solid plan for long-term abundance and security. Take some time to review your budget, set clear financial goals, and identify any areas where you can cut back on expenses or increase your income. Consider investing in your own skills, education, or personal development, as this will pay dividends in the long run. If you've been thinking about starting a side hustle or pursuing a new revenue stream, this is a great time to take action. Trust your instincts and don't be afraid to seek the advice of a financial expert or mentor. Remember, true wealth is not just about material possessions, but about feeling secure, empowered, and aligned with your values. Focus on cultivating a mindset of abundance, gratitude, and generosity, and trust that the universe will support you in creating the financial freedom you desire.

Health:

Capricorn, your health and well-being are in the cosmic spotlight this month, as the planets in your sign encourage you to prioritize self-care, personal growth, and mind-body-spirit alignment. This is an excellent time to recommit to your wellness goals, start a new exercise routine, or explore holistic healing modalities that support your physical, emotional, and spiritual health. With Mars in your 6th house of daily routines, you have the energy and discipline to establish healthy habits that nourish your body and soul. Just be mindful not to overdo it or put too much pressure on yourself – balance is key. Make sure to carve out time for rest, relaxation, and activities that bring you joy and peace. If you've been dealing with any chronic health issues, this is a good time to seek the guidance of a trusted medical professional or alternative healer. Remember, true wellness is about honoring your body's wisdom, listening to your intuition, and treating yourself with love and compassion.

Travel:

January 2025 may not be the most ideal time for long-distance travel, Capricorn, as your focus is more on personal goals, career advancement, and inner growth. However, if you do need to travel for work or other obligations, make sure to plan ahead, double-check all details, and be prepared for potential delays or changes in itinerary. This is a good time to research and book future trips that align with your long-term vision and aspirations. If you're feeling the need for a change of scenery or a mental escape, consider taking a short weekend getaway or exploring a new neighborhood in your city. The key is to find ways to expand your horizons, stimulate your mind, and feed your soul, even if you can't physically travel far. Remember, sometimes the greatest adventures and discoveries happen within, as you journey into the depths of your own psyche and spirituality.

Insights from the Stars:

Capricorn, the celestial energies of January 2025 are urging you to embrace your personal power, step into your authority, and claim your rightful place in the world. With Saturn, your ruling planet, in a supportive aspect to the Sun, Mercury, Venus, and Pluto in your sign, you have the cosmic green light to make your dreams a reality. Trust your inner wisdom, harness your ambition, and don't be afraid to shine your light unapologetically. You are a natural leader, with the discipline, integrity, and resilience to overcome any obstacle and achieve your highest potential. This is a time to let go of self-doubt, limiting beliefs, and the need for external validation. Remember, you are the architect of your own reality, and you have the power to create a life that aligns with your deepest values and desires. Embrace your authentic self, trust the journey, and know that the universe is conspiring in your favor.

Best Days of the Month:

- January 6th: First Quarter Moon in Aries - A powerful day for taking bold action towards your goals and asserting your leadership skills.
- January 13th: Full Moon in Cancer - An emotional time for nurturing your inner world, connecting with loved ones, and creating a sense of home and belonging.
- January 21st: Last Quarter Moon in Libra - An opportunity to find balance, harmony,

and reconciliation in your relationships and partnerships.

- January 29th: New Moon in Capricorn - A potent portal for setting intentions, planting the seeds of your dreams, and recommitting to your personal growth and soul's purpose.

February 2025

Overview Horoscope for the Month:

Welcome to February 2025, Capricorn! This month is all about building on the momentum and breakthroughs you experienced in January, while also focusing on your financial security, personal values, and self-worth. With the Sun illuminating your 2nd house of material resources and possessions, you're called to create a stable foundation for your long-term goals and aspirations. The Full Moon in Leo on February 12th highlights your 8th house of intimacy, shared resources, and personal transformation, bringing powerful insights and revelations about your deepest bonds, psychological patterns, and the ways in which you merge your energy with others. Trust the process of growth and evolution, and know that you have the strength and resilience to face any challenges that may arise.

Love:

In matters of the heart, February 2025 is a month of deepening emotional connections, honest communication, and shared values for you, Capricorn. With Venus transiting your 3rd and 4th houses, you're attracted to partners who stimulate your mind, engage your curiosity, and make you feel emotionally safe and supported. This is a beautiful time to have heartfelt conversations with your loved ones, express your affection and appreciation, and create a nurturing environment for your relationships to thrive. If you're single, you may find yourself drawn to someone who shares your intellectual interests, family values, or cultural background. Take things slow and focus on building a strong foundation of friendship, trust, and mutual respect. If you're in a committed partnership, use this month to deepen your emotional intimacy, communicate your needs and desires openly, and find new ways to support each other's growth and happiness. Remember, true love is a journey of discovery, compromise, and unconditional acceptance.

Career:

Capricorn, your career sector is buzzing with activity and opportunity this month, as Mars energizes your 6th house of work, service, and daily routines. You're feeling motivated, productive, and ready to tackle any challenges that come your way. This is an excellent time to take on new projects, showcase your skills and expertise, and prove your value in the workplace. Your hard work, dedication, and attention to detail will not go unnoticed, and you may receive recognition, a promotion, or a lucrative job offer as a result. Just be mindful of taking on too much at once, as the temptation to overwork or burn yourself out may be strong. Remember to prioritize self-care, delegation, and work-life balance, and don't be afraid to ask for help or support when needed. Trust that your efforts will pay off in the long run, and that your career path is unfolding in perfect divine timing.

Finances:

February 2025 is a powerful month for manifestation, abundance, and financial growth, Capricorn. With the Sun spotlighting your 2nd house of money, possessions, and personal values, you're called to align your spending habits, income streams, and long-term financial goals with your authentic self and life purpose. This is a great time to review your budget, cut back on unnecessary expenses, and invest in your own skills, talents, and personal development. Look for ways to increase your earnings, such as asking for a raise, starting a side hustle, or exploring new revenue streams that align with your passions and expertise. The key is to cultivate a mindset of abundance, gratitude, and self-worth, and to trust that the universe will support you in creating the financial freedom and security you desire. Remember, true wealth is not just about material possessions, but about feeling fulfilled, empowered, and aligned with your deepest values and aspirations.

Health:

Capricorn, your health and well-being are in the cosmic spotlight this month, as the planets encourage you to prioritize self-care, mindfulness, and balance in your daily life. With Mars energizing your 6th house of health, fitness, and routine, you have the motivation and discipline to make positive lifestyle changes that support your physical, emotional, and mental well-being. This is a great time to start a new exercise regimen, explore nutritious meal planning, or incorporate stress-reducing practices like meditation, yoga, or nature walks into your daily schedule. Just be mindful not to overdo it or put too much pressure on yourself to achieve perfection. Remember, true wellness is about listening to your body's wisdom, honoring your unique needs and rhythms, and treating yourself with kindness and compassion. If you've been dealing with any chronic health issues, this is a good time to seek the guidance of a trusted medical professional or holistic healer, and to explore alternative or complementary therapies that resonate with you.

Travel:

February 2025 may bring some unexpected travel opportunities, Capricorn, particularly related to work, education, or personal growth. With Mercury transiting your 3rd house of communication, learning, and short trips, you may find yourself taking impromptu weekend getaways, attending workshops or conferences, or exploring new neighborhoods and communities in your local area. This is a great time to feed your curiosity, expand your mind, and connect with like-minded individuals who share your interests and passions. If you're planning a longer journey, make sure to do your research, read the fine print, and have a backup plan in case of any delays or unforeseen circumstances. Remember, travel is not just about reaching a destination, but about the experiences, insights, and personal growth you gain along the way. Embrace the spirit of adventure, stay open to serendipity, and trust that every journey, whether inner or outer, is an opportunity for self-discovery and transformation.

Insights from the Stars:

Capricorn, the celestial energies of February 2025 are reminding you of the power of authenticity, self-awareness, and emotional intelligence in creating a fulfilling and purposeful life. With Saturn, your ruling planet, in a harmonious aspect to the Sun, Mercury, and Venus this month, you have the wisdom, maturity, and discernment to make choices that align with your highest good and deepest values. Trust your inner guidance system, listen to your intuition, and don't be afraid to set healthy boundaries or say no to people, situations, or commitments that drain your energy or compromise your integrity. Remember, you are the master of your own destiny, and you have the power to create a reality that reflects your true essence and potential. Embrace your unique quirks, honor your sensitive nature, and know that your vulnerability is a strength, not a weakness. The more you can accept and love yourself unconditionally, the more you'll attract relationships, opportunities, and experiences that mirror your inner light and authenticity.

Best Days of the Month:
- February 5th: First Quarter Moon in Taurus - A powerful day for manifestation, abundance, and grounding your dreams in practical action steps.

- February 12th: Full Moon in Leo - A passionate and creative time for expressing your authentic self, celebrating your achievements, and letting your inner child come out to play.
- February 20th: Last Quarter Moon in Sagittarius - An opportunity for release, closure, and tying up loose ends related to travel, education, or personal growth.
- February 27th: New Moon in Pisces - A mystical portal for setting intentions, connecting with your spiritual essence, and surrendering to the flow of the universe.

March 2025

Overview Horoscope for the Month:

Welcome to March 2025, Capricorn! This month promises to be a time of profound transformation, self-discovery, and spiritual awakening. With Saturn, your ruling planet, entering Pisces and your 3rd house of communication, learning, and local community on March 1st, you're being called to expand your mind, challenge your beliefs, and connect with like-minded individuals who share your values and vision. The New Moon in Aries on March 29th falls in your 4th house of home, family, and emotional foundations, bringing powerful opportunities for healing, forgiveness, and new beginnings in your personal life. Trust the process of growth and evolution, and know that you have the strength, resilience, and wisdom to navigate any changes or challenges that may arise.

Love:

In matters of the heart, March 2025 is a month of deep emotional intimacy, spiritual connection, and unconditional love for you, Capricorn. With Venus, the planet of love and relationships, moving through your 4th house of home and family, you're called to create a nurturing, supportive, and loving environment for your closest bonds to thrive. This is a beautiful time to express your affection, appreciation, and vulnerability with your loved ones, and to prioritize quality time, shared experiences, and emotional connection in your relationships. If you're single, you may find yourself attracted to someone who feels like home, who understands your sensitive nature, and who supports your personal growth and healing journey. Trust your intuition, take things slow, and focus on building a strong foundation of trust, respect, and mutual care. If you're in a committed partnership, use this month to deepen your intimacy, communicate your needs and desires openly, and create a shared vision for your future together. Remember, true love is a sacred journey of the heart, and it requires patience, presence, and a willingness to grow and evolve together.

Career:

Capricorn, your career sector is undergoing a powerful transformation this month, as Saturn moves into your 3rd house of communication, learning, and networking. You're being called to expand your skillset, knowledge base, and professional connections, and to align your work with your authentic values and purpose. This is an excellent time to take a course, attend a workshop or conference, or seek out mentorship or guidance from experts in your field. Your ability to communicate effectively, think critically, and collaborate with others will be key to your success and advancement. Just be mindful of taking on too many projects or commitments at once, as the temptation to overextend yourself may be strong. Remember to prioritize balance, self-care, and meaningful work that truly resonates with your soul. Trust that your hard work, dedication, and integrity will pay off in the long run, and that your career path is unfolding in perfect divine timing.

Finances:

March 2025 is a month of financial planning, budgeting, and long-term investments for you, Capricorn. With the Sun illuminating your 3rd house of communication and commerce, you're called to educate yourself about money management, financial literacy, and wealth-building strategies. This is a great time to review your spending habits, create a realistic budget, and explore new ways to increase your income or diversify your revenue streams. Look for opportunities to monetize your skills, talents, and expertise, such as freelancing, consulting, or starting a side business. The key is to align your financial goals with your personal values and life purpose, and to make choices that support your long-term security and abundance. Remember, true wealth is not just about accumulating material possessions, but about feeling fulfilled, empowered, and aligned with your deepest desires and aspirations.

Health:

Capricorn, your health and well-being are in the cosmic spotlight this month, as the planets encourage you to prioritize self-care, mindfulness, and emotional healing. With Saturn moving into your 3rd house of communication and mental processing, you may find yourself dealing with anxious thoughts, self-doubt, or negative self-talk. This is a powerful opportunity to confront your inner critic, challenge your limiting beliefs, and develop a more compassionate and supportive relationship with yourself. Engage in practices that promote relaxation, stress relief, and mental clarity, such as meditation, journaling, or talk therapy. On a physical level, make sure to stay hydrated, eat nourishing foods, and get plenty of rest and exercise. If you've been dealing with any chronic health issues, this is a good time to seek the guidance of a trusted medical professional or holistic healer, and to explore alternative or complementary therapies that support your mind-body-spirit connection.

Travel:

March 2025 may bring some unexpected travel opportunities, Capricorn, particularly related to education, personal growth, or spiritual exploration. With Saturn moving into your 3rd house of short trips and local adventures, you may find yourself taking weekend getaways, exploring new neighborhoods or communities, or attending workshops or retreats that expand your mind and feed your soul. This is a great time to step out of your comfort zone, try new things, and connect with people from different backgrounds or cultures. If you're planning a longer journey, make sure to do your research, read reviews, and have a clear intention or purpose for your trip. Remember, travel is not just about escaping your everyday life, but about discovering new aspects of yourself, broadening your perspective, and finding meaning and connection in the world around you. Embrace the spirit of curiosity, stay open to synchronicity, and trust that every journey, whether inner or outer, is an opportunity for growth, healing, and transformation.

Insights from the Stars:

Capricorn, the celestial energies of March 2025 are inviting you to embrace your inner wisdom, trust your intuition, and align your actions with your soul's purpose. With Saturn, your ruling planet, moving into Pisces and your 3rd house of communication and learning, you're being called to expand your consciousness, challenge your assumptions, and seek out knowledge and experiences that truly resonate with your heart. This is a time to let go of rigid expectations, perfectionist tendencies, or the need to control every outcome, and to surrender to the flow of the universe. Remember, you are a spiritual being having a human experience, and every challenge, setback, or opportunity is a chance to learn, grow, and evolve. Trust that you have the strength, resilience, and inner guidance to navigate any changes or uncertainties that may arise, and that your soul is always leading you towards your highest good and deepest fulfillment.

Best Days of the Month:

- March 6th: First Quarter Moon in Gemini - A great day for learning, networking, and sharing your ideas and insights with others.
- March 14th: Full Moon in Virgo - A powerful time for releasing perfectionism,

embracing self-acceptance, and finding beauty in the imperfections of life.

- March 20th: Sun enters Aries - A new astrological year begins, bringing fresh energy, motivation, and opportunities for personal growth and self-discovery.
- March 29th: New Moon in Aries - A potent portal for setting intentions, planting the seeds of your dreams, and taking bold action towards your goals and desires.

April 2025

Overview Horoscope for the Month:

Capricorn, April 2025 is a month of deep emotional healing, spiritual growth, and personal transformation. With the Sun illuminating your 4th house of home, family, and inner foundations, you're being called to nurture your roots, honor your sensitivity, and create a safe and sacred space for your soul to thrive. The Full Moon in Libra on April 12th highlights your 10th house of career, public image, and long-term goals, bringing powerful opportunities for recognition, advancement, and alignment with your true purpose. Trust the process of growth and evolution, and know that you have the strength, resilience, and wisdom to navigate any changes or challenges that may arise.

Love:

In matters of the heart, April 2025 is a month of emotional intimacy, vulnerability, and unconditional love for you, Capricorn. With Venus, the planet of love and relationships, moving through your 5th house of romance, creativity, and self-expression, you're being called to open your heart, take risks, and let your authentic self shine. This is a beautiful time to prioritize pleasure, passion, and playfulness in your relationships, and to express your affection and appreciation for your loved ones in creative and meaningful ways. If you're single, you may find yourself attracted to someone who shares your values, sparks your curiosity, and brings out the best in you. Trust your intuition, take things slow, and focus on building a strong foundation of friendship, respect, and mutual admiration. If you're in a committed partnership, use this month to deepen your emotional connection, communicate your needs and desires openly, and explore new ways to keep the spark alive. Remember, true love is a journey of the heart, and it requires patience, presence, and a willingness to grow and evolve together.

Career:

Capricorn, your career sector is in the cosmic spotlight this month, as the Full Moon in Libra on April 12th illuminates your 10th house of professional goals, public image, and long-term success. You may find yourself receiving recognition, rewards, or opportunities for advancement that align with your true purpose and values. This is a powerful time to reflect on your achievements, celebrate your progress, and set intentions for the next phase of your career journey. Just be mindful of any power struggles, conflicts, or ego-driven dynamics that may arise, as the Mars-Jupiter conjunction in your 6th house of work and service can heighten tensions and competitiveness. Remember to stay grounded, focused, and true to your integrity, and to prioritize collaboration, teamwork, and the greater good. Trust that your hard work, dedication, and expertise will be valued and rewarded in the long run, and that your career path is unfolding in perfect divine timing.

Finances:

April 2025 is a month of financial planning, budgeting, and long-term investments for you, Capricorn. With the Sun illuminating your 4th house of home and family, you may find yourself focusing on domestic expenses, such as home improvements, renovations, or real estate transactions. This is a great time to review your spending habits, create a realistic budget, and explore ways to increase your savings or invest in your future security. Look for opportunities to generate passive income, such as renting out a property, starting a home-based business, or investing in stocks or mutual funds. The key is to align your financial goals with your personal values and life purpose, and to make choices that support your long-term stability and abundance. Remember, true wealth is not just about accumulating material possessions, but about feeling emotionally fulfilled, spiritually connected, and aligned with your deepest desires and aspirations.

Health:

Capricorn, your health and well-being are undergoing a powerful transformation this month, as the planets encourage you to prioritize self-care, emotional healing, and mind-body-spirit integration. With Chiron, the wounded healer, activating your 4th house of inner foundations and family dynamics, you may find yourself confronting old wounds, traumas, or patterns that have been holding you back from true wellness and vitality. This is a potent opportunity to seek therapy, counseling, or alternative healing modalities that support your emotional and psychological growth. On a physical level, make sure to stay hydrated, eat nourishing foods, and engage in gentle exercise or movement practices that help you release stress and tension. If you've been dealing with any chronic health issues, this is a good time to explore holistic or integrative approaches that address the root causes, rather than just the symptoms. Remember, true healing is a journey of self-discovery, self-acceptance, and self-love, and it requires patience, compassion, and a willingness to let go of what no longer serves you.

Travel:

April 2025 may bring some unexpected travel opportunities, Capricorn, particularly related to family, ancestral roots, or emotional healing. With the North Node activating your 9th house of long-distance journeys, higher education, and spiritual growth, you may feel called to embark on a pilgrimage, retreat, or cultural immersion that expands your mind, opens your heart, and connects you with your soul's purpose. This is a great time to explore your heritage, learn about different philosophies or belief systems, and seek out experiences that challenge your assumptions and broaden your perspective. If you're planning a trip, make sure to do your research, read reviews, and have a clear intention or purpose for your journey. Remember, travel is not just about escaping your everyday life, but about discovering new aspects of yourself, deepening your connection with the world around you, and finding meaning and purpose in the grand adventure of life. Embrace the spirit of curiosity, stay open to synchronicity, and trust that every journey, whether inner or outer, is an opportunity for growth, healing, and transformation.

Insights from the Stars:

Capricorn, the celestial energies of April 2025 are inviting you to embrace your emotional depth, trust your intuition, and align your actions with your soul's purpose. With the Sun, Mercury, and Venus activating your 4th house of home, family, and inner foundations, you're being called to nurture your roots, honor your sensitivity, and create a safe and sacred space for your heart to heal and your spirit to soar. This is a time to let go of any masks, defenses, or barriers that have been keeping you from authentic connection and vulnerability, and to open yourself up to the transformative power of love, compassion, and self-acceptance. Remember, you are a divine being of light and love, and your deepest wounds and shadows are portals to your greatest strengths and gifts. Trust that you have the courage, resilience, and inner guidance to navigate any changes or challenges that may arise, and that your soul is always leading you towards your highest good and deepest fulfillment.

Best Days of the Month:

- April 4th: Saturn sextile Uranus - A powerful day for innovation, progress, and breaking free from limitations or obstacles.

- April 12th: Full Moon in Libra - A potent portal for harmony, balance, and aligning your personal and professional goals with your highest values and aspirations.
- April 16th: Mercury enters Aries - A great time for new ideas, fresh perspectives, and bold communication in your personal and professional life.
- April 20th: Sun enters Taurus - A new solar cycle begins, bringing stability, security, and a focus on your material and emotional foundations.

May 2025

Overview Horoscope for the Month:

Capricorn, May 2025 is a month of personal growth, self-expression, and creative exploration. With the Sun illuminating your 5th house of romance, passion, and authenticity, you're being called to let your unique light shine, pursue your heart's desires, and take risks in the name of love and joy. The New Moon in Taurus on May 26th activates your 5th house as well, bringing powerful opportunities for new beginnings, fresh starts, and bold self-expression. Trust the process of growth and evolution, and know that you have the courage, resilience, and creativity to manifest your dreams and desires.

Love:

In matters of the heart, May 2025 is a month of passion, playfulness, and emotional authenticity for you, Capricorn. With Venus, the planet of love and relationships, moving through your 6th house of daily routines and service, you're being called to find beauty, pleasure, and connection in the simple, everyday moments of life. This is a beautiful time to express your affection and appreciation for your loved ones through acts of kindness, thoughtful gestures, and quality time together. If you're single, you may find yourself attracted to someone who shares your values, supports your goals, and brings a sense of stability and security to your life. Trust your intuition, take things slow, and focus on building a strong foundation of friendship, respect, and mutual care. If you're in a committed partnership, use this month to deepen your emotional intimacy, communicate your needs and desires openly, and find new ways to keep the spark of romance alive. Remember, true love is a journey of the heart, and it requires patience, presence, and a willingness to grow and evolve together.

Career:

Capricorn, your career sector is undergoing a powerful transformation this month, as the Lunar Eclipse in Scorpio on May 12th activates your 11th house of networking, teamwork, and long-term goals. You may find yourself letting go of old attachments, limitations, or collaborations that no longer align with your true purpose and values, and embracing new opportunities, connections, and visions for your professional future. This is a potent time to reflect on your achievements, reassess your priorities, and set intentions for the next phase of your career journey. Just be mindful of any power struggles, conflicts, or hidden agendas that may arise, as the eclipse energy can bring buried tensions or secrets to the surface. Remember to stay grounded, focused, and true to your integrity, and to prioritize transparency, fairness, and the greater good. Trust that your hard work, dedication, and expertise will be recognized and rewarded in divine timing, and that your career path is unfolding in perfect alignment with your soul's purpose.

Finances:

May 2025 is a month of financial planning, budgeting, and long-term investments for you, Capricorn. With the Sun and New Moon activating your 5th house of creativity, self-expression, and entrepreneurship, you may find yourself exploring new ways to monetize your talents, skills, and passions. This is a great time to start a side hustle, launch a creative project, or invest in your own business or brand. Look for opportunities to generate multiple streams of income, such as selling your art or crafts online, offering freelance services, or teaching classes or workshops. The key is to align your financial goals with your personal values and life purpose, and to make choices that support your long-term security and abundance. Remember, true wealth is not just about accumulating material possessions, but about feeling creatively fulfilled, emotionally satisfied, and aligned with your deepest desires and aspirations.

Health:

Capricorn, your health and well-being are in the cosmic spotlight this month, as the planets encourage you to prioritize self-care, pleasure, and vitality. With Mars, the planet of action and energy, moving through your 8th house of transformation, intimacy, and deep healing, you may find yourself confronting old wounds, traumas, or patterns that have been holding you back from true wellness and aliveness. This is a potent opportunity to engage in deep emotional work, such as therapy, journaling, or shamanic healing, and to release any toxic habits, relationships, or beliefs that no longer serve your highest good. On a physical level, make sure to stay hydrated, eat nourishing foods, and engage in activities that bring you joy, pleasure, and a sense of flow. If you've been dealing with any chronic health issues, this is a good time to explore alternative or holistic approaches that address the mind-body-spirit connection, such as acupuncture, reiki, or energy healing. Remember, true healing is a journey of self-discovery, self-acceptance, and self-love, and it requires patience, compassion, and a willingness to embrace your shadows as well as your light.

Travel:

May 2025 may bring some exciting travel opportunities, Capricorn, particularly related to creativity, self-expression, or personal growth. With Jupiter, the planet of expansion and abundance, activating your 6th house of daily routines and work, you may find yourself taking a business trip, attending a conference or workshop, or exploring new ways to bring more adventure and inspiration into your everyday life. This is a great time to break out of your comfort zone, try new things, and seek out experiences that broaden your mind, open your heart, and feed your soul. If you're planning a vacation, consider destinations that offer a mix of relaxation, culture, and natural beauty, such as a yoga retreat in Bali, a art history tour in Italy, or a wilderness adventure in Costa Rica. Remember, travel is not just about escaping your everyday life, but about discovering new aspects of yourself, deepening your connection with the world around you, and finding meaning and purpose in the grand adventure of life. Embrace the spirit of curiosity, stay open to synchronicity, and trust that every journey, whether inner or outer, is an opportunity for growth, healing, and transformation.

Insights from the Stars:

Capricorn, the celestial energies of May 2025 are inviting you to embrace your creative power, trust your heart's desires, and align your actions with your soul's purpose. With the Sun, Mercury, and Venus activating your 5th house of self-expression, passion, and authenticity, you're being called to let your unique light shine, take risks in the name of love and joy, and pursue the dreams and desires that make you come alive. This is a time to let go of any self-doubt, fear, or limitations that have been holding you back from your true potential, and to embrace the magic, mystery, and adventure of life. Remember, you are a divine creator, with the power to manifest your reality through your thoughts, beliefs, and actions. Trust that the universe is always conspiring in your favor, and that your deepest desires are a reflection of your soul's purpose. Have faith in yourself, follow your bliss, and know that you are loved, supported, and guided every step of the way.

Best Days of the Month:

- May 4th: Saturn sextile Uranus - A powerful day for innovation, progress, and breaking free from limitations or obstacles.
- May 12th: Full Moon Lunar Eclipse in Scorpio - A potent portal for deep

transformation, emotional healing, and releasing what no longer serves your highest good.

- May 16th: Mercury enters Taurus - A great time for practical planning, financial management, and grounding your ideas in tangible reality.
- May 26th: New Moon in Taurus - A beautiful opportunity for new beginnings, fresh starts, and planting the seeds of your dreams and desires.

June 2025

Overview Horoscope for the Month:

Welcome to June 2025, Capricorn! This month promises to be a time of personal growth, self-improvement, and service to others. With the Sun illuminating your 6th house of health, work, and daily routines, you're being called to focus on your well-being, productivity, and the ways in which you can make a positive impact in the world. The New Moon in Cancer on June 25th activates your 7th house of partnerships and relationships, bringing powerful opportunities for new beginnings, deepening connections, and aligning yourself with people who support your highest good. Trust the process of growth and evolution, and know that you have the discipline, dedication, and integrity to create a life of balance, purpose, and fulfillment.

Love:

In matters of the heart, June 2025 is a month of emotional intimacy, vulnerability, and compromise for you, Capricorn. With Venus, the planet of love and relationships, moving through your 7th house of partnerships, you're being called to focus on the needs, desires, and well-being of your significant other. This is a beautiful time to express your affection, appreciation, and support for your partner, and to find ways to deepen your connection through shared activities, meaningful conversations, and acts of kindness. If you're single, you may find yourself attracted to someone who is emotionally mature, reliable, and committed to personal growth. Trust your intuition, take things slow, and focus on building a strong foundation of friendship, trust, and mutual respect. Remember, true love is a journey of the heart, and it requires patience, presence, and a willingness to meet each other halfway.

Career:

Capricorn, your career sector is in the cosmic spotlight this month, as the Sun and Mercury activate your 6th house of work, service, and daily responsibilities. You may find yourself taking on new projects, learning new skills, or seeking ways to improve your efficiency and productivity in the workplace. This is a great time to focus on the details, organize your schedule, and streamline your processes to ensure maximum success and satisfaction. Just be mindful of any tendencies towards perfectionism, overwork, or self-criticism, as the Mars-Neptune square on June 18th can heighten feelings of confusion, doubt, or overwhelm. Remember to take breaks, prioritize self-care, and ask for help when needed. Trust that your hard work, dedication, and expertise will be recognized and rewarded in divine timing, and that your career path is unfolding in perfect alignment with your soul's purpose.

Finances:

June 2025 is a month of financial planning, budgeting, and practical decision-making for you, Capricorn. With the Sun and Mercury illuminating your 6th house of work and daily routines, you may find yourself focusing on ways to increase your income, reduce your expenses, or invest in your long-term security. This is a great time to review your spending habits, create a realistic budget, and explore opportunities for additional sources of income, such as freelance work, side hustles, or passive investments. The key is to align your financial goals with your personal values and life purpose, and to make choices that support your overall well-being and happiness. Remember, true wealth is not just about accumulating material possessions, but about feeling secure, empowered, and fulfilled in all areas of your life.

Health:

Capricorn, your health and well-being are in the cosmic spotlight this month, as the Sun, Mercury, and Venus activate your 6th house of health, fitness, and daily habits. You're being called to focus on your physical, mental, and emotional well-being, and to make choices that support your vitality, balance, and overall quality of life. This is a great time to start a new exercise routine, try a healthy diet, or engage in activities that bring you joy, relaxation, and stress relief. Just be mindful of any tendencies towards overindulgence, addiction, or escapism, as the Mars-Neptune square on June 18th can heighten feelings of temptation, confusion, or self-sabotage. Remember to listen to your body's wisdom, practice moderation, and seek support when needed. Trust that your commitment to self-care, self-love, and self-improvement will pay off in the long run, and that your health is your greatest wealth.

Travel:

June 2025 may bring some unexpected travel opportunities, Capricorn, particularly related to work, service, or personal growth. With Mars, the planet of action and energy, moving through your 9th house of adventure, higher learning, and spiritual seeking, you may find yourself taking a business trip, attending a conference or workshop, or exploring new ways to expand your mind, broaden your horizons, and deepen your connection with the world around you. This is a great time to step out of your comfort zone, try new things, and seek out experiences that challenge your assumptions, inspire your curiosity, and awaken your sense of wonder. If you're planning a vacation, consider destinations that offer a mix of relaxation, education, and cultural immersion, such as a language immersion program in Spain, a yoga teacher training in India, or a volunteer trip to a developing country. Remember, travel is not just about escaping your everyday life, but about discovering new aspects of yourself, learning from different perspectives, and finding meaning and purpose in the grand adventure of life.

Insights from the Stars:

Capricorn, the celestial energies of June 2025 are inviting you to embrace your inner wisdom, trust your intuition, and align your actions with your highest values and aspirations. With Saturn, your ruling planet, forming a supportive sextile to Uranus on June 4th, you have the opportunity to break free from old patterns, limitations, or fears, and to embrace a new level of innovation, progress, and personal freedom. This is a time to let go of any beliefs, habits, or relationships that no longer serve your growth and evolution, and to open yourself up to the infinite possibilities of the universe. Remember, you are a powerful creator, with the ability to manifest your dreams and desires through your thoughts, words, and actions. Trust that the challenges and opportunities you face are all part of your soul's journey, and that you have the strength, resilience, and wisdom to navigate them with grace and purpose. Have faith in yourself, stay true to your path, and know that you are divinely guided and supported every step of the way.

Best Days of the Month:
- June 4th: Saturn sextile Uranus - A powerful day for innovation, progress, and breaking free from limitations or obstacles.
- June 11th: Full Moon in Sagittarius - A beautiful time for expansion, exploration, and aligning your actions with your highest truth and wisdom.
- June 18th: Jupiter sextile Chiron - A healing and transformative aspect that supports emotional healing, spiritual growth, and the resolution of past wounds or traumas.

- June 25th: New Moon in Cancer - A potent portal for new beginnings, fresh starts, and setting intentions related to your relationships, emotional well-being, and inner sense of security.

July 2025

Overview Horoscope for the Month:

Capricorn, July 2025 is a month of personal growth, self-reflection, and inner transformation. With the Sun illuminating your 7th house of partnerships and relationships until July 22nd, you're being called to focus on the balance, harmony, and mutual support in your closest connections. The Full Moon in Capricorn on July 9th brings a powerful opportunity for self-realization, emotional authenticity, and the release of any patterns or beliefs that no longer serve your highest good. Trust the process of growth and evolution, and know that you have the wisdom, integrity, and resilience to create a life of purpose, fulfillment, and deep connection.

Love:

In matters of the heart, July 2025 is a month of emotional intimacy, vulnerability, and compromise for you, Capricorn. With Venus, the planet of love and relationships, moving through your 8th house of deep bonding and transformation, you're being called to explore the shadows, desires, and fears that shape your intimate connections. This is a profound time to have honest conversations with your partner about your needs, boundaries, and expectations, and to find ways to deepen your trust, commitment, and mutual understanding. If you're single, you may find yourself attracted to someone who challenges you to grow, heal, and embrace your authentic self. Trust your intuition, take your time, and focus on building a connection based on shared values, emotional maturity, and a willingness to do the inner work. Remember, true love is a journey of the soul, and it requires courage, compassion, and a commitment to your own personal evolution.

Career:

Capricorn, your career sector is undergoing a powerful transformation this month, as the Full Moon in your sign on July 9th illuminates your 10th house of public image, professional goals, and long-term success. You may find yourself reaching a significant milestone, receiving recognition for your hard work, or facing a critical decision that will shape the direction of your career path. This is a time to trust your inner guidance, stay true to your values, and make choices that align with your authentic purpose and passions. Just be mindful of any tendencies towards workaholism, perfectionism, or self-doubt, as the Sun-Pluto opposition on July 17th can heighten feelings of intensity, pressure, or power struggles. Remember to prioritize self-care, set healthy boundaries, and seek support when needed. Trust that your dedication, expertise, and integrity will be rewarded in divine timing, and that your career is an expression of your soul's unique gifts and talents.

Finances:

July 2025 is a month of financial planning, budgeting, and long-term strategizing for you, Capricorn. With Mercury, the planet of communication and commerce, moving through your 8th house of shared resources and investments, you may find yourself focusing on ways to increase your financial security, pay off debts, or create a more equitable distribution of wealth in your relationships. This is a great time to have honest conversations with your partner or family members about your financial goals, concerns, and expectations, and to explore ways to support each other's economic well-being. Just be mindful of any tendencies towards secrecy, control, or mistrust, as the Mercury-Pluto opposition on July 22nd can heighten feelings of suspicion, jealousy, or manipulation. Remember to practice transparency, fairness, and open communication in all your financial dealings, and to make choices that align with your values and long-term vision. Trust that your resourcefulness, practicality, and wise management will lead to greater abundance, stability, and peace of mind in the long run.

Health:

Capricorn, your health and well-being are in the cosmic spotlight this month, as the planets encourage you to focus on your emotional, psychological, and spiritual healing. With Chiron, the wounded healer, stationing retrograde in your 4th house of home, family, and inner foundations on July 30th, you may find yourself revisiting old wounds, traumas, or family patterns that have shaped your sense of safety, belonging, and self-worth. This is a profound opportunity to seek therapy, counseling, or alternative healing modalities that support your inner child, your emotional resilience, and your ability to create a nurturing and supportive environment for yourself and your loved ones. On a physical level, make sure to prioritize rest, relaxation, and stress management, as the Mars-Uranus square on July 7th can heighten feelings of tension, anxiety, or impulsivity. Remember to listen to your body's wisdom, practice self-compassion, and seek help when needed. Trust that your commitment to your own healing, growth, and self-love will ripple out to create more loving, authentic, and fulfilling relationships in all areas of your life.

Travel:

July 2025 may bring some unexpected travel opportunities, Capricorn, particularly related to personal growth, spiritual seeking, or emotional healing. With the North Node moving through your 9th house of adventure, higher learning, and foreign cultures, you may feel called to embark on a transformative journey, attend a life-changing workshop or retreat, or explore new ways of expanding your mind, heart, and soul. This is a powerful time to step out of your comfort zone, challenge your assumptions and beliefs, and open yourself up to the wisdom and beauty of different perspectives and ways of being. If you're planning a trip, consider destinations that offer a mix of natural wonder, cultural richness, and sacred sites, such as a meditation retreat in the mountains of Tibet, a shamanic journey in the Amazon rainforest, or a pilgrimage to the holy lands of Jerusalem. Remember, travel is not just about escaping your everyday life, but about discovering the depths of your own being, connecting with the greater web of life, and finding your place in the grand mystery of existence.

Insights from the Stars:

Capricorn, the celestial energies of July 2025 are inviting you to embrace your inner authority, trust your soul's wisdom, and align your actions with your deepest values and aspirations. With Saturn, your ruling planet, forming a supportive trine to the North Node on July 21st, you have the opportunity to step into your true power, leadership, and purpose, and to make choices that support your long-term growth, success, and fulfillment. This is a time to let go of any fears, doubts, or limitations that have held you back from claiming your rightful place in the world, and to embrace the unique gifts, talents, and experiences that make you who you are. Remember, you are a wise, capable, and resilient being, with the strength, integrity, and determination to overcome any obstacle and achieve any goal you set your mind to. Trust that the challenges and opportunities you face are all part of your soul's journey, and that you have the courage, grace, and support to navigate them with wisdom, compassion, and purpose. Have faith in yourself, stay true to your path, and know that you are a vital part of the greater tapestry of life, weaving your thread of love, light, and service into the world.

Best Days of the Month:

- July 9th: Full Moon in Capricorn - A powerful day for self-realization, emotional authenticity, and releasing what no longer serves your highest good.
- July 21st: Saturn trine North Node - A supportive aspect for stepping into your true power, leadership, and purpose, and making choices that align with your long-term growth and success.
- July 23rd: Sun enters Leo - A time of creative self-expression, heart-centered living, and joyful celebration of your unique gifts and talents.
- July 28th: Venus enters Virgo - A beautiful opportunity for practical acts of love and service, and for bringing more order, beauty, and efficiency to your relationships and daily life.

August 2025

Overview Horoscope for the Month:

Welcome to August 2025, Capricorn! This month promises to be a time of deep transformation, emotional healing, and spiritual growth. With the Sun illuminating your 8th house of intimacy, shared resources, and psychological depths, you're being called to confront your shadows, fears, and desires, and to embrace the power of vulnerability, trust, and surrender. The New Moon in Leo on July 24th and the Full Moon in Aquarius on August 9th bring powerful opportunities for letting go of old patterns, beliefs, and attachments, and for birthing a new version of yourself that is more authentic, compassionate, and aligned with your soul's purpose. Trust the process of death and rebirth, and know that you have the strength, courage, and resilience to navigate any challenges or changes that may arise.

Love:

In matters of the heart, August 2025 is a month of deep emotional connection, passionate intensity, and transformative healing for you, Capricorn. With Venus, the planet of love and relationships, moving through your 8th and 9th houses this month, you're being called to explore the depths of your desires, fears, and attachments, and to open yourself up to new ways of giving and receiving love. This is a powerful time to have honest conversations with your partner about your needs, boundaries, and expectations, and to find ways to deepen your intimacy, trust, and mutual understanding. If you're single, you may find yourself attracted to someone who challenges you to grow, heal, and embrace your authentic self. Trust your intuition, take your time, and focus on building a connection based on shared values, emotional maturity, and a willingness to do the inner work. Remember, true love is a journey of the soul, and it requires courage, compassion, and a commitment to your own personal evolution.

Career:

Capricorn, your career sector is undergoing a powerful transformation this month, as Mars and Venus join forces in your 8th house of shared resources, power dynamics, and deep psychological shifts. You may find yourself confronting old fears, doubts, or limitations that have held you back from fully expressing your talents, skills, and leadership potential. This is a time to trust your inner guidance, stay true to your values, and make bold moves that align with your authentic purpose and passions. Just be mindful of any tendencies towards control, manipulation, or self-sabotage, as the Mars-Venus conjunction can heighten feelings of intensity, desire, and competition. Remember to practice self-care, set healthy boundaries, and seek support when needed. Trust that your hard work, dedication, and integrity will be rewarded in divine timing, and that your career is an expression of your soul's unique gifts and purpose.

Finances:

August 2025 is a month of deep financial transformation, metaphorical death and rebirth, and the unleashing of your true abundance and prosperity, Capricorn. With the Sun, Mercury, and Venus activating your 8th house of shared resources, investments, and psychological blocks around money, you're being called to confront any fears, limiting beliefs, or unhealthy patterns that have prevented you from fully owning your worth and receiving the financial flow you deserve. This is a powerful time to do some deep inner work around your relationship with money, to release any guilt, shame, or scarcity mentality, and to embrace a new paradigm of sufficiency, gratitude, and generosity. You may also find yourself dealing with themes of inheritance, taxes, debts, or joint finances this month, which can bring up intense emotions or power struggles. Remember to practice clear communication, fair negotiation, and emotional maturity in all your financial dealings, and to make choices that align with your values and long-term vision. Trust that as you heal your relationship with money, you open yourself up to new streams of abundance, prosperity, and fulfillment.

Health:

Capricorn, your health and well-being are undergoing a deep transformation this month, as the planets encourage you to release old toxins, patterns, and limitations, and to embrace a new level of vitality, resilience, and wholeness. With the Sun, Mercury, and Venus activating your 8th house of deep healing, regeneration, and metamorphosis, you're being called to confront any physical, emotional, or spiritual imbalances that have been holding you back from optimal health and happiness. This is a powerful time to seek out alternative or holistic healing modalities, such as acupuncture, energy work, or psychotherapy, and to explore the mind-body-soul connection in your wellness journey. You may also find yourself dealing with themes of addiction, obsession, or compulsion this month, which can be challenging but also transformative. Remember to practice self-compassion, seek support when needed, and trust in your body's innate wisdom and resilience. As you release what no longer serves you, you create space for new levels of vitality, joy, and aliveness to emerge.

Travel:

August 2025 may bring some intense but transformative travel experiences for you, Capricorn, particularly related to deep healing, spiritual awakening, or emotional catharsis. With Mars and Venus joining forces in your 8th house of death, rebirth, and metamorphosis, you may feel called to embark on a journey that challenges you to confront your fears, shadows, and limiting beliefs, and to embrace a new level of courage, authenticity, and freedom. This could be a powerful time to attend a transformational workshop or retreat, to explore sacred sites or natural wonders that hold deep meaning for you, or to embark on a solo journey of self-discovery and soul-searching. Just be mindful of any tendencies towards recklessness, impulsivity, or escapism, as the Mars-Venus conjunction can heighten feelings of intensity, desire, and restlessness. Remember to practice self-care, set clear intentions, and trust in the journey, even if it feels uncomfortable or uncertain at times. Trust that every experience, whether challenging or blissful, is an opportunity for growth, healing, and awakening.

Insights from the Stars:

Capricorn, the celestial energies of August 2025 are inviting you to embrace the power of surrender, trust, and transformation. With the Sun, Mercury, and Venus activating your 8th house of death, rebirth, and deep psychological shifts, you're being called to let go of any old identities, patterns, or attachments that no longer serve your highest good, and to allow yourself to be transformed by the fires of change and growth. This is a time to trust in the intelligence of the universe, to surrender to the flow of life, and to have faith that every ending is also a new beginning. Remember that you are a resilient, powerful, and eternal being, with the strength, wisdom, and courage to navigate any challenges or transitions that may arise. Trust in your soul's journey, stay open to the mysteries and miracles of existence, and know that you are always guided, protected, and loved by the divine forces of the cosmos.

Best Days of the Month:

- August 9th: Full Moon in Aquarius - A powerful day for releasing old patterns, beliefs, and limitations, and for embracing a new level of freedom, innovation, and authenticity.

- August 11th: Mercury stations direct - A time for clarity, insight, and forward momentum, particularly related to communication, learning, and self-expression.

- August 18th: Mars and Venus conjunct in Leo - A passionate, creative, and transformative aspect that heightens desire, courage, and self-expression, but also requires emotional maturity and healthy boundaries.

- August 30th: Jupiter biquintile Pluto - A rare and powerful aspect that supports deep psychological healing, spiritual transformation, and the emergence of new levels of wisdom, power, and purpose..

September 2025

Overview Horoscope for the Month:

Capricorn, September 2025 is a month of expansion, growth, and new horizons. With the Sun illuminating your 9th house of adventure, higher learning, and spiritual seeking, you're being called to broaden your mind, explore new frontiers, and align your actions with your deepest truth and highest purpose. The New Moon in Virgo on September 21st brings a powerful opportunity to set intentions related to travel, education, publishing, or entrepreneurship, while the Full Moon in Pisces on September 7th invites you to release any fears, illusions, or limiting beliefs that have held you back from fully embodying your wisdom, faith, and creativity. Trust the journey of growth and evolution, and know that you have the vision, resilience, and determination to create a life of meaning, purpose, and endless possibility.

Love:

In matters of the heart, September 2025 is a month of adventure, romance, and spiritual connection for you, Capricorn. With Venus, the planet of love and relationships, moving through your 9th and 10th houses this month, you're being called to expand your horizons, explore new dimensions of love and intimacy, and align your partnerships with your highest values and aspirations. If you're single, you may find yourself attracted to someone who shares your love of learning, travel, or personal growth, and who inspires you to be your best self. Be open to long-distance connections, cross-cultural romances, or unconventional arrangements that challenge your assumptions and beliefs about love. If you're in a committed relationship, this is a beautiful time to plan a romantic getaway, take a class or workshop together, or explore new ways of deepening your emotional, intellectual, and spiritual bond. Remember, true love is an adventure of the heart, mind, and soul, and it requires courage, curiosity, and a willingness to step outside your comfort zone.

Career:

Capricorn, your career sector is on fire this month, as Mars enters your 10th house of public image, professional goals, and long-term success on

September 22nd. You're feeling ambitious, driven, and ready to take bold action towards your dreams and aspirations. This is a powerful time to put yourself out there, showcase your talents and skills, and make moves that align with your authentic purpose and leadership potential. Just be mindful of any tendencies towards aggression, competitiveness, or burnout, as Mars can sometimes bring up feelings of anger, frustration, or impatience. Remember to practice self-care, collaborate with others, and balance your hard work with rest and play. Trust that your dedication, expertise, and integrity will be recognized and rewarded in divine timing, and that your career is a vehicle for expressing your unique gifts and making a positive impact in the world.

Finances:

September 2025 is a month of financial growth, expansion, and opportunity for you, Capricorn. With Jupiter, the planet of abundance and prosperity, moving through your 8th house of shared resources, investments, and deep psychological shifts, you're being called to embrace a new level of financial flow, collaboration, and empowerment. This is a powerful time to explore new streams of income, negotiate better deals or contracts, or invest in ventures that align with your values and long-term vision. You may also find yourself dealing with themes of inheritance, taxes, debts, or joint finances this month, which can bring up intense emotions or power dynamics. Remember to practice clear communication, fair negotiation, and emotional maturity in all your financial dealings, and to make choices that support your overall well-being and happiness. Trust that as you heal your relationship with money and embrace a mindset of abundance, you open yourself up to new levels of prosperity, fulfillment, and joy.

Health:

Capricorn, your health and well-being are in a state of expansion, growth, and vitality this month, as the planets encourage you to embrace a more holistic, adventurous, and spiritually aligned approach to wellness. With the Sun, Mercury, and Venus activating your 9th house of higher learning, travel, and personal growth, you're being called to explore new philosophies, practices, and experiences that support your physical, emotional, and spiritual health. This is a great time to try a new yoga or meditation class, experiment with international cuisines or healing modalities, or embark on a wellness retreat or pilgrimage that nourishes your body, mind, and soul. You may also find yourself drawn to studies or teachings that expand your understanding of health, healing, and the nature of reality. Remember to approach your wellness journey with a sense of curiosity, open-mindedness, and self-compassion, and to trust in the innate wisdom and intelligence of your body. As you align your lifestyle with your deepest values and highest truth, you create a foundation of vitality, resilience, and radiance that will serve you for years to come.

Travel:

September 2025 is a month of exciting travel opportunities and adventures for you, Capricorn, as the celestial energies align to support your exploration of new horizons, cultures, and ways of being. With the Sun, Mercury, and Venus illuminating your 9th house of foreign lands, higher education, and spiritual seeking, you may find yourself called to embark on a transformative journey that expands your mind, opens your heart, and enriches your soul. This could be a great time to plan a study abroad program, a volunteer trip, or a pilgrimage to a sacred site that holds deep meaning for you. You may also be drawn to travel experiences that challenge your assumptions, beliefs, and comfort zones, such as a wilderness adventure, a cultural immersion, or a spiritual retreat. Whatever form your travels take, approach them with a sense of curiosity, humility, and openness to the unknown.

Trust that every encounter, whether challenging or blissful, is an opportunity for growth, learning, and self-discovery. As you explore the world around you, you also explore the depths of your own being, and discover new dimensions of your potential, purpose, and place in the greater web of life.

Insights from the Stars:

Capricorn, the celestial energies of September 2025 are inviting you to embrace the power of faith, wisdom, and alignment with your highest truth. With Jupiter, the planet of expansion and growth, moving through your 8th house of deep transformation and regeneration, you're being called to let go of any old beliefs, patterns, or limitations that have kept you from fully embodying your authentic self and living your soul's purpose. This is a time to trust in the intelligence of the universe, to surrender to the flow of life, and to have faith that every experience, whether challenging or blissful, is guiding you towards your highest good and greatest evolution. Remember that you are a wise, powerful, and eternal being, with access to infinite resources, guidance, and support from the divine realms. Trust in your own inner knowing, stay open to the signs and synchronicities of the universe, and know that you are always being led towards your deepest fulfillment and most radiant expression of your true self.

Best Days of the Month:

- September 3rd: Jupiter trine North Node - A powerful aspect that supports spiritual growth, karmic healing, and alignment with your soul's purpose and path.
- September 7th: Full Moon in Pisces - A mystical and emotionally charged lunation that invites deep release, surrender, and connection with the divine realms.
- September 21st: New Moon in Virgo - A potent portal for setting intentions, refining your skills and routines, and aligning your actions with your highest values and goals.
- September 22nd: Mars enters Capricorn - A dynamic and ambitious transit that empowers you to take bold action, assert your leadership, and make strides towards your long-term aspirations.

October 2025

Overview Horoscope for the Month:

Welcome to October 2025, Capricorn! This month promises to be a time of career advancement, public recognition, and personal transformation. With the Sun illuminating your 10th house of professional goals, ambition, and status until October 22nd, you're being called to step into your power, claim your authority, and make bold moves towards your long-term aspirations. The New Moon in Libra on October 21st brings a powerful opportunity to set intentions related to your career, reputation, and leadership potential, while the Full Moon in Aries on October 6th invites you to release any fears, doubts, or self-limiting beliefs that have held you back from fully expressing your unique talents and gifts. Trust the process of growth and evolution, and know that you have the strength, resilience, and determination to achieve your highest goals and make a positive impact in the world.

Love:

In matters of the heart, October 2025 is a month of depth, intensity, and transformation for you, Capricorn. With Venus, the planet of love and relationships, moving through your 10th and 11th houses this month, you're being called to align your partnerships with your deepest values, aspirations, and sense of purpose. If you're in a committed relationship, this is a powerful time to have honest conversations with your partner about your shared goals, dreams, and visions for the future. You may find yourselves working together on a project or cause that is meaningful to you both, or exploring new ways of supporting each other's growth and success. If you're single, you may find yourself attracted to someone who shares your ambition, integrity, and commitment to making a difference in the world. Be open to connections that challenge you to step into your power, express your authenticity, and embrace your unique path and purpose. Remember, true love is a sacred bond that empowers you to be your best self and make a positive impact in the world.

Career:

Capricorn, your career sector is on fire this month, as the Sun, Mercury, and Venus activate your 10th house of professional goals, public image, and long-term success. You're feeling focused, driven, and ready to take your work and leadership to the next level. This is a powerful time to put yourself out there, showcase your talents and accomplishments, and make bold moves towards your dreams and aspirations. You may find yourself in the spotlight, receiving recognition or rewards for your hard work and dedication, or being offered new opportunities or promotions that align with your long-term vision. Just be mindful of any tendencies towards workaholism, perfectionism, or self-doubt, as the Full Moon in Aries on October 6th can bring up fears or insecurities related to your worth and value. Remember to practice self-care, set healthy boundaries, and surround yourself with supportive people who believe in you and your potential. Trust that your passion, expertise, and commitment to excellence will take you far, and that your career is a vehicle for expressing your unique gifts and making a positive impact in the world.

Finances:

October 2025 is a month of financial growth, expansion, and opportunity for you, Capricorn. With Jupiter, the planet of abundance and prosperity, moving through your 9th house of higher learning, travel, and entrepreneurship, you're being called to explore new ways of generating income, building wealth, and aligning your resources with your values and vision. This is a powerful time to invest in your education, skills, or personal development, or to consider starting your own business or venture that allows you to share your knowledge and expertise with others. You may also find yourself attracted to financial opportunities or investments that have a global or philanthropic dimension, such as socially responsible funds, international trade, or eco-friendly enterprises. Remember to approach your financial decisions with a sense of integrity, wisdom, and long-term vision, and to trust your intuition and inner guidance when it comes to money matters. As you align your resources with your deepest values and highest aspirations, you create a foundation of abundance, prosperity, and purpose that will serve you for years to come.

Health:

Capricorn, your health and well-being are in a state of balance, vitality, and resilience this month, as the planets support your efforts to prioritize self-care, mindfulness, and holistic wellness. With Mars, the planet of energy and action, moving through your 12th house of rest, retreat, and spiritual healing, you're being called to slow down, turn inward, and listen to the wisdom of your body and soul. This is a powerful time to engage in practices that promote relaxation, stress relief, and inner peace, such as meditation, yoga, or nature walks. You may also find yourself drawn to alternative or complementary healing modalities that address the root causes of any physical or emotional imbalances, such as acupuncture, energy work, or herbal medicine. Remember to approach your health journey with a sense of compassion, patience, and trust in the innate intelligence of your body. As you honor your needs for rest, nourishment, and self-love, you create a foundation of vitality, harmony, and radiance that will support you in all areas of your life.

Travel:

October 2025 may bring some exciting travel opportunities and adventures related to your career, education, or personal growth, Capricorn. With Jupiter, the planet of expansion and exploration, moving through your 9th house of foreign lands, higher learning, and spiritual seeking, you may find yourself called to embark on a journey that broadens your mind, opens your heart, and expands your horizons. This could be a great time to attend a conference or workshop in your field, to study abroad or pursue an advanced degree, or to take a sabbatical or career break that allows you to explore new cultures, ideas, and ways of being. You may also be drawn to travel experiences that have a purpose or mission beyond mere pleasure or escape, such as a volunteer trip, a cultural exchange, or a pilgrimage to a sacred site. Whatever form your travels take, approach them with a sense of curiosity, openness, and willingness to learn and grow. Trust that every encounter, whether challenging or inspiring, is an opportunity for self-discovery, transformation, and alignment with your highest path and purpose.

Insights from the Stars:

Capricorn, the celestial energies of October 2025 are inviting you to embrace your power, purpose, and potential as a leader, change-maker, and visionary. With Saturn, your ruling planet, forming a supportive trine to the North Node in Aries on October 21st, you're being called to step into your authority, claim your destiny, and make bold moves towards your long-term goals and aspirations. This is a time to trust in your inner guidance, to align your actions with your deepest values and highest truth, and to have faith in the unfolding of your unique path and purpose. Remember that you are a wise, capable, and resilient being, with the strength, integrity, and determination to overcome any challenge and achieve any dream. Trust in the journey of your soul, stay open to the lessons and opportunities of each moment, and know that you are always being guided and supported by the loving intelligence of the universe.

Best Days of the Month:
- October 6th: Full Moon in Aries - A powerful lunation that invites you to release fears, doubts, and self-limiting beliefs, and to embrace your courage, confidence, and authentic self-expression.
- October 16th: Mercury enters Scorpio - A deep and transformative transit that supports honest communication, psychological insight, and the unveiling of hidden truths and desires.
- October 21st: New Moon in Libra - A potent portal for setting intentions related to your career, reputation, and leadership potential, and for aligning your goals with your values and vision.
- October 21st: Saturn trine North Node - A supportive aspect that empowers you to claim your authority, align with your destiny, and make bold moves towards your long-term aspirations and purpose.

November 2025

Overview Horoscope for the Month:

Capricorn, November 2025 is a month of social connection, humanitarian pursuits, and personal liberation. With the Sun illuminating your 11th house of friendships, community, and hopes and dreams, you're being called to expand your network, collaborate with like-minded individuals, and work towards a vision of a better world. The New Moon in Scorpio on November 20th brings a powerful opportunity to set intentions related to your social life, group activities, and collective endeavors, while the Full Moon in Taurus on November 5th invites you to release any attachments, possessions, or values that no longer serve your highest good. Trust the process of growth and evolution, and know that you have the wisdom, compassion, and innovative spirit to create positive change in your life and in the world.

Love:

In matters of the heart, November 2025 is a month of unconventional romance, emotional freedom, and authentic connection for you, Capricorn. With Venus, the planet of love and relationships, moving through your 11th and 12th houses this month, you're being called to embrace a more liberated, unconditional, and spiritual approach to love and intimacy. If you're in a committed relationship, this is a powerful time to break free from any patterns, roles, or expectations that have limited your growth and happiness as a couple. You may find yourselves exploring new ways of relating, communicating, and supporting each other's individuality and independence. If you're single, you may find yourself attracted to someone who is unique, progressive, and emotionally mature, and who shares your vision of a more just, compassionate, and awakened world. Be open to connections that challenge you to expand your mind, open your heart, and embrace your authentic self. Remember, true love is a sacred journey of two souls walking together, supporting each other's freedom, growth, and highest potential.

Career:

Capricorn, your career sector is undergoing a powerful transformation this month, as the planetary energies support your efforts to align your work with your deepest values, passions, and sense of purpose. With Mars, the planet of action and ambition, moving through your 12th house of spirituality, surrender, and inner wisdom, you're being called to let go of any goals, projects, or commitments that no longer resonate with your soul's calling. This is a time to trust your intuition, listen to your inner guidance, and make space for new opportunities and directions that feel more authentic and fulfilling. You may find yourself drawn to careers or ventures that have a humanitarian, creative, or spiritual dimension, such as social activism, the arts, or holistic healing. Remember to approach your professional path with a sense of detachment, flexibility, and openness to change, and to trust that the universe is guiding you towards your highest potential and purpose.

Finances:

November 2025 is a month of financial collaboration, innovation, and social responsibility for you, Capricorn. With Jupiter, the planet of abundance and expansion, moving through your 10th house of career and public reputation, you're being called to align your financial goals with your values, integrity, and desire to make a positive impact in the world. This is a powerful time to explore new income streams, partnerships, or investments that support your long-term vision and contribute to the greater good. You may find yourself attracted to socially conscious businesses, ethical investing, or philanthropic endeavors that allow you to use your resources to create positive change. Remember to approach your financial decisions with a sense of discernment, wisdom, and generosity, and to trust that the more you give, the more you receive. As you align your wealth with your highest purpose and values, you create a foundation of prosperity, fulfillment, and social impact that will benefit you and others for years to come.

Health:

Capricorn, your health and well-being are in a state of renewal, rejuvenation, and spiritual alignment this month, as the planets support your efforts to prioritize self-care, inner peace, and holistic healing. With the Sun and Mercury activating your 11th house of social connection and community, you may find yourself drawn to group activities, classes, or events that promote physical, emotional, and mental well-being, such as yoga retreats, meditation circles, or wellness workshops. You may also feel inspired to join or create a support group or community that shares your health goals and values, and that provides a sense of belonging, accountability, and motivation. Remember to approach your wellness journey with a sense of curiosity, experimentation, and self-compassion, and to listen to the unique needs and rhythms of your body, mind, and soul. As you nurture your own health and happiness, you become a beacon of inspiration and healing for others, and contribute to the collective well-being of your community and the world.

Travel:

November 2025 may bring some unexpected travel opportunities and adventures related to your social life, community involvement, or humanitarian pursuits, Capricorn. With Uranus, the planet of change and innovation, moving through your 5th house of creativity, self-expression, and adventure, you may find yourself called to embark on a journey that awakens your sense of wonder, joy, and spontaneity. This could be a great time to take a trip with friends or like-minded individuals, to attend a festival or conference that celebrates your passions and values, or to explore a destination that is known for its progressive culture, artistic scene, or natural beauty. You may also be drawn to travel experiences that have a social or environmental impact, such as a volunteer vacation, an eco-tour, or a cultural exchange program. Whatever form your travels take, approach them with a sense of openness, flexibility, and willingness to step outside your comfort zone. Trust that every encounter, whether planned or serendipitous, is an opportunity for growth, connection, and alignment with your highest path and purpose.

Insights from the Stars:

Capricorn, the celestial energies of November 2025 are inviting you to embrace your role as a visionary, change-maker, and leader in creating a more just, compassionate, and awakened world. With Pluto, the planet of power and transformation, stationed direct in your 2nd house of values, resources, and self-worth on October 13th, you're being called to align your personal desires and ambitions with your soul's deepest truth and purpose. This is a time to let go of any fears, limitations, or attachments that have kept you from fully embodying your authentic power and potential, and to trust in the unfolding of your unique path and destiny. Remember that you are a wise, courageous, and resilient being, with the strength, integrity, and determination to overcome any obstacle and create positive change in your life and in the world. Trust in the journey of your soul, stay open to the lessons and opportunities of each moment, and know that you are always being guided and supported by the loving intelligence of the universe.

Best Days of the Month:

- November 5th: Full Moon in Taurus - A powerful lunation that invites you to release attachments, possessions, and values that no longer serve your highest good, and to embrace a more liberated, authentic, and abundant way of being.
- November 7th: Uranus sextile Neptune - A rare and transformative aspect that supports spiritual awakening, creative inspiration, and the dissolution of old patterns and beliefs that have limited your growth and happiness.
- November 20th: New Moon in Scorpio - A potent portal for setting intentions related to your social life, group activities, and humanitarian pursuits, and for aligning your actions with your deepest values and highest vision.
- November 27th: Saturn semi-sextile Chiron - A healing and empowering aspect that supports the integration of past wounds, the development of inner wisdom, and the alignment of your personal goals with your soul's purpose and path.

December 2025

Overview Horoscope for the Month:

Welcome to December 2025, Capricorn! This month promises to be a time of spiritual growth, inner reflection, and emotional healing. With the Sun illuminating your 12th house of solitude, surrender, and divine connection, you're being called to slow down, turn inward, and listen to the whispers of your soul. The New Moon in Sagittarius on December 19th brings a powerful opportunity to set intentions related to your spiritual practice, creative expression, and inner peace, while the Full Moon in Gemini on December 4th invites you to release any thoughts, beliefs, or communication patterns that no longer serve your highest good. Trust the process of letting go, and know that you have the wisdom, compassion, and faith to navigate any challenges or uncertainties that may arise.

Love:

In matters of the heart, December 2025 is a month of emotional depth, spiritual intimacy, and unconditional love for you, Capricorn. With Venus, the planet of love and relationships, moving through your 12th house of divine connection and universal love, you're being called to embrace a more compassionate, forgiving, and transcendent approach to your romantic life. If you're in a committed relationship, this is a powerful time to release any grudges, resentments, or expectations that have limited your ability to love and be loved fully. You may find yourselves exploring new ways of communicating, connecting, and supporting each other's spiritual growth and emotional healing. If you're single, you may find yourself attracted to someone who is kind, empathetic, and spiritually awake, and who shares your desire for a love that is pure, unconditional, and divinely guided. Be open to connections that challenge you to open your heart, forgive your past, and trust in the power of love to heal and transform. Remember, true love is a sacred gift from the universe, and it requires surrender, grace, and a willingness to love without conditions or expectations.

Career:

Capricorn, your career sector is undergoing a powerful transformation this month, as the planetary energies support your efforts to align your work with your soul's deepest calling and purpose. With Mars, the planet of action and ambition, moving through your 1st house of self and identity, you're being called to take bold steps towards your personal goals and aspirations, and to assert your unique talents, skills, and leadership potential. This is a time to trust your instincts, follow your passions, and make career choices that feel authentic, fulfilling, and aligned with your highest values and vision. You may find yourself drawn to careers or projects that have a creative, spiritual, or humanitarian dimension, such as the arts, philanthropy, or personal development. Remember to approach your professional path with a sense of courage, integrity, and self-belief, and to trust that the universe is guiding you towards your true purpose and potential.

Finances:

December 2025 is a month of financial healing, surrender, and divine providence for you, Capricorn. With the Sun and Mercury activating your 12th house of spirituality, letting go, and higher power, you're being called to release any fears, anxieties, or limiting beliefs around money and abundance, and to trust in the infinite supply and support of the universe. This is a powerful time to practice gratitude, generosity, and faith in the face of any financial challenges or uncertainties, and to believe that all your needs and desires will be met in perfect timing and divine order. You may find yourself attracted to philanthropic causes, charitable giving, or tithing as a way of aligning your resources with your spiritual values and beliefs. Remember to approach your financial life with a sense of surrender, trust, and inner peace, and to know that true wealth comes from within, and is measured by the love, joy, and fulfillment you experience in your life.

Health:

Capricorn, your health and well-being are in a state of healing, renewal, and spiritual alignment this month, as the planets support your efforts to prioritize self-care, emotional release, and inner peace. With Chiron, the wounded healer, stationed direct in your 4th house of home, family, and emotional foundations on December 30th, you're being called to address any past traumas, family patterns, or emotional wounds that have impacted your sense of safety, belonging, and self-worth. This is a powerful time to seek therapy, counseling, or alternative healing modalities that support your emotional and psychological well-being, and to create a nurturing and supportive environment for your mind, body, and soul. You may also find yourself drawn to practices that promote relaxation, stress relief, and inner calm, such as meditation, prayer, or spending time in nature. Remember to approach your healing journey with a sense of patience, self-compassion, and trust in the wisdom of your body and soul, and to know that you are always loved, supported, and guided by the universe.

Travel:

December 2025 may bring some profound travel experiences and opportunities related to your spiritual growth, creative expression, or emotional healing, Capricorn. With Neptune, the planet of imagination, inspiration, and divine connection, moving through your 3rd house of communication, learning, and short trips, you may find yourself called to embark on a journey that expands your mind, opens your heart, and awakens your sense of wonder and creativity. This could be a great time to attend a spiritual retreat, creative workshop, or healing seminar in a beautiful and inspiring location, or to take a short trip to a place that holds special meaning or significance for you. You may also be drawn to travel experiences that involve poetry, music, art, or other forms of creative expression, as a way of tapping into your inner muse and connecting with the divine. Whatever form your travels take, approach them with a sense of openness, surrender, and trust in the journey, and know that every experience is an opportunity for growth, healing, and alignment with your highest path and purpose.

Insights from the Stars:

Capricorn, the celestial energies of December 2025 are inviting you to embrace the power of surrender, faith, and divine connection. With Jupiter, the planet of expansion, wisdom, and higher truth, moving through your 12th house of spirituality, transcendence, and letting go, you're being called to release any attachments, expectations, or fears that have kept you from fully trusting in the wisdom and guidance of the universe. This is a time to deepen your spiritual practice, connect with your inner wisdom, and allow yourself to be guided by the loving intelligence of the cosmos. Remember that you are a divine being of light and love, with access to infinite grace, support, and protection from the unseen realms. Trust in the journey of your soul, stay open to the signs and synchronicities of the universe, and know that you are always being led towards your highest good and greatest purpose.

Best Days of the Month:

- December 4th: Full Moon in Gemini - A powerful lunation that invites you to release any thoughts, beliefs, or communication patterns that no longer serve your highest good, and to embrace a more authentic, clear, and compassionate way of expressing yourself.

- December 10th: Neptune Direct - A subtle but profound shift that supports spiritual awakening, creative inspiration, and the dissolving of illusions and limiting beliefs.

- December 19th: New Moon in Sagittarius - A potent portal for setting intentions related to your spiritual growth, creative expression, and inner peace, and for aligning your actions with your deepest truth and highest wisdom.

- December 30th: Chiron Direct - A healing and empowering shift that supports the integration of past wounds, the development of inner wisdom, and the alignment of your personal goals with your soul's purpose and path.

Made in the USA
Thornton, CO
11/22/24 18:04:06